HOME SERIES

HOME SERIES
ARCHITECTS' HOUSES

BETA-PLUS

CONTENTS

P. 4-5, 6 and 8
A house characterised by the
pure lines typical of the
architect Pascal Van der Kelen.

INTRODUCTION

W ho doesn't dream of pushing open the door to the home of a professional architect or interior designer? How does their design vision translate in their own private space? What does their refuge from the world look like? How do they come up with a design for their home which is well thought out when they are no longer bound by their clients' requirements? What imaginative solutions have they created for their homes in response to the specific challenges of their surroundings?

This volume invites us to take a look at interior design from a new angle and enjoy a private and privileged insight into some top of the range interior designs. It features a selection of homes which showcase the work of around ten architects and interior designers. Whether it be the materials, the dynamics of the space or the imaginative layout, these homes are abound with original ideas and stunning aesthetics. From clever use of light to glass walls, modular spaces, removable partition walls and radical interior design choices, these architects have used every ounce of their experience and made creative use of techniques and materials. Their homes are places where they can experiment. This volume is therefore a source of inspiration and an insight into modern interior design, which illustrates the sensitivity of these professionals to their surroundings and their achievements. Whether their ultra-contemporary property was built for them or by them, or whether they have completely redesigned an old or uncharacteristic apartment, each architect or designer's project epitomises a futuristic vision and a love of contemporary features, which are defined, where necessary, by any existing historical features.

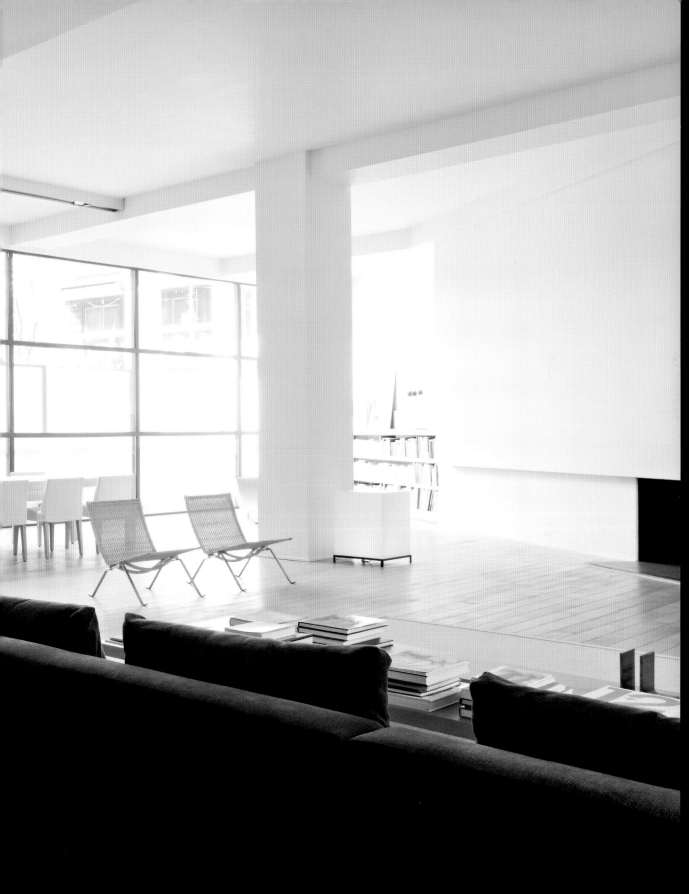

NEW LEASE OF LIFE FOR A

CHARACTER PROPERTY IN GENEVA

T his apartment in a seventeenth century apartment block in the heart of Geneva's old town epitomises the Lodge concept by Welton Design.

Property developer Brigitte Boiron and interior designer John-Paul Welton have given this character property a new lease of life. The choice of furniture with contemporary lines gives the apartment a distinctive style. It is the perfect city pad from which to enjoy life in Geneva.

The radical black and white décor makes for an emphatic and timeless combination.

P. 12-15
The floor in the living room is made from polished concrete. Linen curtains by Osborne & Little.
Round wenge table from the "Sensation" collection by Welton Design. Leather settee from the "Samira" collection by Welton Design. The white gloss console table is also by Welton Design ("Harmony" collection). Cowhide armchair from the "Alana" collection by Welton Design.

Note...

> The rustic ceiling has been modernised with a coat of white gloss paint, making the room feel brighter. Preserving this historic feature gives the room character and originality.

> The partition wall has a niche cut through it and does not reach to the ceiling; this gives the room a relaxed feel and ensures that the line of vision is not broken.

P. 16-19
The kitchen floor is also made of polished concrete. Arclinea kitchen (by Ambiance Cuisine) with a refrigerator by Siemens and oven and hob by Brandt.

The wardrobe was custom-made by Luc Obersson. The bed is from the "Como" collection by Welton Design.

Both the floor and walls are finished with polished concrete. The bathroom fittings are by Dornbracht (Mem collection) and the bath is by Laufen.

PURE LINES

T his architect's home is built on a left-over triangular plot on an established housing development. It is situated close to a busy road, but also offers superb views over some beautiful agricultural land.

These were key factors in the design of this project by the architecture firm Hans Verstuyft.

The dark façade blends beautifully into the natural surroundings. The concrete plinths give the overall design an elegant character.

The in-built terrace complete with fireplace creates a sense of intimacy.

The large private hallway offers views in all directions. The surrounding countryside is brought right into the building, creating an intense feeling of being outside. The concrete structure is exposed both on the exterior — with the thick paving slabs and cornices — and the interior, where the patterning of the exposed concrete casing slabs on the ceiling enhances the design.

P. 26-27
The minimalist interior design and pure lines mean that art and architecture complement one another beautifully.

The surrounding countryside is a striking feature. The simple furniture contrasts beautifully with the timeless architecture. A classic Fortuny lamp takes pride of place.

Note...

> The minimalist interior design ensures that the striking spaces and architecture are not compromised; there are no curtains or ostentatious décor. The furniture is plain and in keeping with the house.

P. 29-31
Just like a camp fire, the real wood fire is lit on the floor.
When all the doors are open, the different spaces blend smoothly together. The exposed patterning of the concrete ceiling reinforces the consistency of the design.

The landing has a sensual atmosphere and evokes a feeling of calm: it is a natural space with an abundance of natural light and rugged natural stone.

Large windows also feature here, this time with a guard rail. Each bedroom has its own balcony.

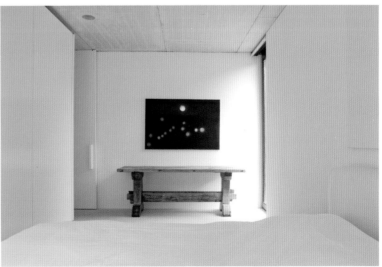

The sense of tranquillity is at its height in the bathroom. The tall bath is large enough for two people. The custom-made wash basin is made of natural stone.
Indirect lighting gives the room a touch of warmth. The double window can also be opened to give the delightful sensation of bathing in the open air.

LINES AND ANGLES
IN THE MAURES MOUNTAINS

N ot content to simply design his private home, the architect Marc Lust also put his professional work to one side for three years in order to build it with his own hands.

Situated in the Maures Mountains – a small chain of mountains which runs between Hyères and Fréjus (in the department of Var) – the property reflects Lust's contemporary architectural style: it is characterised by austere lines and angles and the use of light is a fundamental element in the creation of a pure and classic space.

A straight 25 m walkway leads up to the main entrance. Through the double oak doors is the central, open-air patio, onto which all of the main rooms in the house open out.

Note...

> Different levels give the patio a dynamic feel and create a sense of space.

> A sort of plant sculpture, the olive tree forms the centrepiece for this ultra contemporary space.

P. 40-45
Terraces on different levels link the house and the swimming pool. The pool house with its solarium terrace and covered barbeque area rounds off the poolside design beautifully. Natural stone, teak and white gravel are used to distinguish between walkways and areas for relaxation. Sweeping pieces of canvas provide shade and give the space a relaxed feel.
The outside areas have been designed as if they were actual rooms in the house.

P. 46-49

The high ceilings, white walls and large flagstones made of light natural stone help to give the rooms a tranquil atmosphere.

The interior design by Joëlle Lust is chic, refined and pure without being austere.

Note...

> The suspended partition wall above the fireplace can also be used as a projection screen.

> The large, sliding windows which open out onto the swimming pool and the patio ensure a seamless dialogue between the exterior and the interior.

The study opens out onto the patio and also offers a view into the dining room, living room and swimming pool through the extensive glass windows.

The central island, which contains the walk-in wardrobe, separates the bedroom from the bathroom. The large shower area is decorated with pebbles and the bath looks out over the surrounding forest.

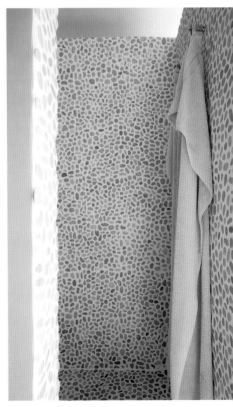

A PRIVATE TOUR OF THE HOME

OF GÉRARD FAIVRE

The renowned architect and interior designer Gérard Faivre splits his professional work between his two homes in Provence and Paris.

In Saint-Germain-des-Prés, one of the most beautiful districts in Paris, Faivre has uncovered a modern apartment to fit his requirements, right opposite the Jardin du Luxembourg.

The space has high ceilings, is bathed in light and, despite being in the heart of the city, is surrounded by plenty of green space where he can recharge his batteries after his endless toing and froing between building sites, modern art exhibitions and other professional events.

P. 58-63
Gérard Faivre knows the design classics by heart. In his private apartment he has created ample space for armchairs, designed notably by Paolo Navone, Poltrona Frau and Le Corbusier, a desk by Cassina and more.

Note...

> This design dares to use stark contrasts: traditional wood panelling sits side-by-side with designer furniture – a tricky, yet successful, combination.

Decoration idea

> Painting the ceiling using a dark shade gives the room a greater sense of intimacy and originality.

> Extremely discreet storage units are hidden in the mirror behind the settee. This mirrored wall balances out the room's very high ceilings by creating the impression of greater space.

> Natural elements are incorporated into the interior design: the chosen colours, plant fibre materials and woods make for a calming décor which is far removed from the chaos of the city.

THE HOME-COME-WORKSHOP

OF A PASSIONATE ARCHITECT

This townhouse, which dates back to 1884, had hardly been altered over the years. As a result, the original structures and décor had been preserved but substantial restoration work and a complete rethink of design techniques were required in order to complete its transformation.

The property has been transformed into the home-come-workshop of the architect Anne Derasse. A true haven of tranquillity in the heart of the capital, it comprises a front house, a garden — planted with old fruit trees, box trees and clipped hornbeams — and a rear house with an old pigeon loft.

In restoring the property and creating its interior design, Anne Derasse constantly sought to preserve its charming original features while at the same time complementing them with unique and timeless contemporary features.

The successful renovation of this nineteenth century house uses contemporary techniques which showcase the building's architectural heritage.

The conservatory leans against the rear façade wall, which serves as a backdrop for the grape vine. Unlike the other lower walls which have been left chalk coloured, the façade has been painted entirely in grey anthracite right up to the roof of the house, in order to enhance the shadows and light patterns created.

Note...

> Grey anthracite is a daring colour for the façade but it complements the splendid patterns created by the elegant period cement floor tiles. The result is a timeless conservatory.

The original *faux bois* four-part doors which lead from the living room to the conservatory have been cleaned and polished.

The cement tiles and faux marble are original.
The staircase balusters have been painted faux black to provide a contrast on all floors of the house.

The sofa, which was designed by Anne Derasse, is upholstered in bronze coloured velvet. The low table in front of the settee was designed by Carlo Colombo for Zanotta (leather top with graphite base).
The occasional table with rosewood top and gloss anthracite base was designed by Pierre Chareau for the Ecart collection. Standing lamp also from the Ecart collection. The low bookcases were designed by Anne Derasse. Works of art by Dotrement, Alechinsky and Tremlett.

Note...

> Rarely encountered colours such as the rich green-bronze paint used for the walls give the room an elegant quality. The floors have been stained an ebony colour to complement this shade.

> A new use has been created for the fireplace, with the hearth serving as a small storage area.

The pattern in the centre of the ceiling, the friezes on the lower panelling and the arabesque gilding on the doors are all original and have been professionally restored. The painting entitled "La Seigneurie" is by Rose & Partners. The table is a prototype by Lebrun. Chairs by Lissoni for Cappellini.

A corrugated chair made from cardboard by Frank Gehry.

The faux marble in the entrance hall has been cleaned and polished. Console table by Antonio Citterio for Maxalto. The painting above the console table is by Geoffroy de Volder.

Note...

> Respect for the original features: the furniture is deliberately simple to ensure that it does not detract from the beautiful wall and ceiling decoration.

The annexe designed by the architect Y. Franchimont, and the terraces which level out the sloping garden which extends as far as the rear house. Kitchen furnishings designed by Anne Derasse.

The rear house has two floors and serves as an office-come-workshop. Samples of materials, documentation and colour charts are labelled and stored methodically.
Table created by Citterio for B&B Italia. The armchairs date back to the 1930s. Magazine racks by Xavier Lust and draw unit by Jules Wabbes.

P. 80-81
The first floor is designed as a suite with a bedroom, walk-in wardrobe, lounge and bathroom.

The walk-in wardrobe and bathroom were designed by Anne Derasse.

The lounge which leads off the bedroom
is furnished with bookshelves by
Citterio (Maxalto) and a sofa. Coffee
table designed by Carlo Colombo for
Zanotta. Linen curtains and work of art
by Bram van Velde.

TRANSFORMATION

OF A 1960s HOME

T his 1960s property has been transformed into an architect's home by the company AID-architects. The company has refurbished it and added a wing for the children on the roof.

All of the original internal walls were built in triplicate within a uniform lattice of brick columns. The doors and cupboards blend into the house's architecture.

The architecture resembles that of a simple building game, while the interior is a delicate puzzle which fits perfectly inside.

With its flawless proportions, the arrangement of the columns and the use of wood, an undeniable sense of calm pervades throughout this home.

P. 86-89

So as not to upset the perfect synergy between the spacing and arrangement of the columns, it was decided that the addition of the upper floor must be as discrete as possible. Small electric shutters built into the façade create superb perspectives and delightful patterns of light. In summer, the outside terrace which adjoins the kitchen transforms into an additional living space. The garden beautifully complements and completes the design of this architect's house.

The interior design has been stripped right back to basics with the choice of light-coloured and natural materials. Highly original furniture, which is full of character, contrasts with the nonchalant design of the custom-made pieces.

Note...

> A space bathed in light: the brightness of the space is enhanced by the use of light coloured materials such as the bleached parquet floor and the beige and greyish-beige coloured furniture. This soft monochrome colour scheme gives the space a cosy atmosphere despite the stripped-back, contemporary architecture.

The compact kitchen is the very heart of the house.

Decoration idea

> The kitchen is completely open plan, yet it remains discrete thanks to the absence of any tall cupboards and the fact that the storage units and appliances are all built into one wall.

> There is no break in the flooring; the parquet floor has been treated to ensure its resistance and extends right into the kitchen, which further increases the sense of space.

Like the rest of the house, the parent's bedroom is a serene space where interior and exterior are in constant dialogue with one another.

The first floor landing houses a study corner for the parents and children.

The discrete in-built cupboards in the walls of the dressing room mean that this is also a relaxing space with a view.

WORKING FROM HOME

IN COMPLETE TRANQUILLITY

More and more people are choosing to bring their place of work into their home. The premises of the Reginald Schellen architecture firm is an excellent example of how professional and private life can be combined in a building with timeless architecture.

The project had two aims: firstly to incorporate the private home and the architecture firm offices into a single building; and secondly to create an interior design for these two very distinct areas. The two areas are separated by a large central interior wall made of glass, hung on both sides with an enormous 4 x 4 metre work by the painter Stefan Annerel. Here, private and professional life rub shoulders every day.

The entrance area has an extremely simple design which makes clever use of open and closed spaces.

The offices are spread over two floors and situated on the road-facing side of the building. Cedar wood slats filter and protect the eyes against the incoming sunlight.

A hardwood walkway gently slopes up from the road to the entrance.

Situated on the edge of a wood, the tranquil garden is extremely simple in design and easy to maintain. House, terrace, garden and wood blend together naturally.
The south-facing rear façade is entirely open and overlooks the garden.

The façade which overlooks the garden is made entirely of glass, establishing a visual connection between the interior and exterior. The overhanging brickwork of the rear façade, with its first floor terraces, prevents the area from becoming excessively hot in summer.

The private residence and offices share a common entrance hall which features a large revolving door. The porch roof is symmetrical in design.

Daylight penetrates the house through a glass strip in the roof and illuminates the work of art.

Note...

> The staircase combines design and functionality. Despite the discrete reassuring handrail, it retains the illusion of being elevated and extremely light. Leaning against the glass wall it appears to be floating and is transformed into a form of sculpture.

> The stunning interior glass wall both separates and joins the private and professional spaces. The enormous work of art protects both sides from prying eyes without destroying the connection between them.

The small lounge area, central dining area and kitchen all flow together. The kitchen was designed by the interior designer Linda Coart of Reginald Schellen.
The sinks have been built into the enormous elongated black granite work top. All the kitchen utensils are hidden behind sliding doors.

All the private living areas look out over the neighbouring wood. The varying heights of the open spaces are a real trademark of the designer.

AN ARCHITECT'S LOFT CONVERSION

T he interior designer Pieter Vandenhout's third floor loft conversion in an industrial building epitomises his vision of architecture, design and "mild" restorations.

The space is characterised by a striking and uncompromising décor: the floors, ceiling and walls are all decorated in the same colour, erasing the boundaries between them. Paradoxically, this space gives you a sense of being protected, no doubt conveyed by the "box" effect and the tones of the colours that have been selected.

In the background are two decorative sixteenth century pieces from Italy. According to Vandenhout, these are not masterpieces, but it is precisely this imperfection which the interior designer finds intriguing.
Just in front is a design classic: the Lounge & Ottoman created by Charles and Ray Eames.

Despite the refined contemporary setting, the vast spaces give the building the appearance of an historic construction.

Note...

> Despite its cold grey anthracite colour, the floor retains a warm appearance thanks to its many varying shades. This warmth is replicated on the walls where effects such as textured lime render or tadelakt create an almost sensual finish.

> The choice of rustic furniture and course materials, such as the rough linen cover on the settee, mixed in with design classics creates a unique atmosphere (see following pages).

P. 108-111
The standing lamp by Mariano Fortuny is still a design icon. Here it is combined with Wassilly chairs created by Marcel Breuer and cosy settees by Axel Vervoordt. The floor is made of grey poly cement.

Pieter Vandenhout's private loft conversion creates synergies between old and new influences, simplicity, purity and an absence of limits and boundaries. The result is a feeling of timelessness.

Pieter Vandenhout's work pays no heed to current trends. His company creates designs which go beyond the here and now, based on the intrinsic importance of the functionality of each building. The contradiction between old and new ceases to exist.

HOME SERIES

Volume 28 : ARCHITECTS' HOUSES

The reports in this book are selected from the Beta-Plus collection of home-design books: www.betaplus.com
They have been compiled in a special series by Le Figaro in French language: Ma Déco.

Copyright © 2010 Beta-Plus Publishing / Le Figaro
Originally published in French language

PUBLISHER
Beta-Plus Publishing
Termuninck 3
B – 7850 Enghien
Belgium
www.betaplus.com
info@betaplus.com

TEXT
Alexandra Druesne

PHOTOGRAPHY
Jo Pauwels

DESIGN
Polydem - Nathalie Binart

TRANSLATIONS
Txt-Ibis

ISBN: 978-90-8944-082-2

P. 118-119 and 122-123
Two views of the private home of architect Pascal Van der Kelen.

P. 120-121
A house created by the architect Marc Corbiau.

P. 124-125
A project by Martine Cammaert.

P. 126-127
A design created by the Olivier Dwek architecture firm.